ALONG MOUNTAIN TRAILS
(AND IN BOGGY MEADOWS)

A Guide to Northern
Rocky Mountain
Wildflowers & Berries
2nd Edition

Photos and text
by
Doreen Marsh Dorward

Illustrations and text
by
Sally Randall Swanson

Boggy Meadows Press
Ketchum, Idaho

FRONT COVER PHOTO
Showy Penstemon

BACK COVER PHOTO
Indian Paintbrush
Elephant Heads

Doreen and Sally

Library of Congress Catalog Card Number: 98-068522

ISBN: 1-56044-234-4

Published by The Boggy Meadows Press
Ketchum, Idaho

For extra copies, contact:
The Boggy Meadows Press
Box 5129
Ketchum, ID 83340

Second edition, first printing

Manufactured in Korea

DEDICATION

This book is dedicated to those who blazed the mountain trails and first saw these wildflowers, to those who hike with us today and take delight in finding them, and to those who will follow and have yet to discover the wonders of Rocky Mountain wildflowers.

PREFACE

We have written this book with the hope that it will help you to identify flowers you come across while hiking along mountain trails or slogging through boggy meadows. For ease in identification, we have arranged the flowers by colors. When a species grows in more than one color, we have placed it with the most commonly found color. We have included a glossary, illustrated plant parts, and family characteristics to aid you in your identification.

Please be aware that flowers bloom at different times and can be different sizes according to altitude, climatic conditions, and geographic locations. Flowers featured in this book can be found growing in high deserts, on mountains, along streamsides and lakes, and in alpine areas above the timberline.

Since there are hundreds of species growing in the Northern Rocky Mountains, it is impossible to include them all in one small guide that can be easily carried. Some areas may have different common names for the same flower. We have used the name most commonly used in our area.

We hope that you will come to appreciate these beautiful wildflowers in their natural surroundings and will leave them, not only for others to enjoy, but also to give them an opportunity to reproduce themselves.

ABOUT THE AUTHORS

Doreen Dorward was born in Sebastopol, California (north of San Francisco), and has a B.A. and teaching credential from Stanford University and Dominican College. She is a well-known photographer and author of several books and magazine articles. For the past twelve years, she has conducted classes in wildflower identification and photography in Sun Valley. A Ketchum area resident for over twenty years, her Idaho roots go back to her grandfather, who was one of the first settlers in the Twin Falls Tract in 1904. He had previously come west with his family on the Oregon Trail.

Sally Swanson was born in Petoskey, Michigan, and developed a love of the outdoors and wildflowers in early childhood. She grew up in tropical Florida and Tahiti, the woods of Maine and Michigan, and the desert of Arizona. A graduate of Stanford University, she now lives in Ketchum, Idaho, where from early spring to late fall she can be found hiking the mountains with sketchpad and watercolors always in her backpack.

GLOSSARY

Alternate: growing singly on a stem at differing points (not opposite)

Annual: a plant that has a life cycle of one year

Anther: the part of a stamen where pollen is produced

Axil: the angle where a leaf joins the stem

Basal: attaching to the stem near the ground

Biennial: a plant with a life cycle of at least two years, usually blooming in the second

Bract: a modified leaf growing just below the flower

Bulb: the underground swollen part of a stem, composed of succulent leaf-bases

Calyx: all the sepals of a flower; usually green, but can be other colors also

Cleft: when a leaf margin is indented halfway or more to the center rib

Composite: a flower consisting of either outer ray flowers or center disk flowers or both

Compound: a leaf divided into two or more sections

Corm: enlarged underground base of a stem, which is solid, not layered like a bulb

Corolla: all the petals of a flower

Corymb: a flower cluster with stems growing from many different points

Cyme: loose branches of flowers growing opposite on a stem

Deciduous: plants that shed their leaves after each growing season

Disk flowers: the small, tubular flowers in the center of some composites

Filament: the slender stalk that supports an anther

Hybrid: an offspring that is derived from the pollination of two different species

Involucre: the bracts surrounding a flower cluster

Lanceolate: shaped like a lance or spear

Linear: long and narrow, grasslike

Lobed: with slightly indented margins (not as deep as cleft)

Nectar: a flower secretion that attracts insects, and aids pollination

Node: the swollen place on a stem from where leaves or buds grow

Opposite: attaching to the stem at the same point

Ovary: the female part of a flower, where seeds develop after pollination occurs

Ovate: egg-shaped, broader at the base

Palmate: with veins and lobes that spread out from a central point

Panicle: loose branches of flowers alternating up a stem

Perennial: a plant living for an indefinite length of time, usually blooming every year

Perfoliate: a leaf attaching to a stem that appears to pierce it through the center

Petal: a single section of the corolla; may be separate or joined at the base, usually colored

Petiole: the stalk that attaches a leaf to the stem

Pinnate: describes a leaf with many opposite leaflets sharing a common stem

Pistil: the entire female part of a flower, comprising the stigma, style, and ovary

Pollen: the fine powder produced by the male anther, which fertilizes the ovary of a flower

Raceme: many flowers attached to a main stalk, each with its own stem

Ray flowers: the outer flowers surrounding disk flowers in some composites

Rhizome: a horizontal, underground stem

Runner: a shoot that runs along the ground and sends roots down to produce new plants

Saprophyte: a plant that lacks chlorophyll, and lives on decaying organic material

Sepal: a single section of the outer calyx; usually green, but can be other colors

Serrated: when a leaf edge is sharply toothed, like a saw
Sheath: the tubular base of a leaf that surrounds the stem
Shrub: a low, woody plant with several branches growing from a base
Species: a category used to classify plants that are of the same type
Spike: many flowers attached to a main stalk with no stems
Spur: a tubular projection found in some flowers
Stamen: the male part of a flower, composed of the anther and filament
Stigma: the top of the female style, where male pollen collects during the fertilization process
Stipules: small, leaflike parts that grow where leaves join the stem
Style: the slender stalk that connects the stigma with the ovary; the middle part of the pistil
Succulent: a think, fleshy plant that stores moisture
Taproot: the thick, straight, main root growing downward from a plant
Toothed: describes a jagged edge on the margin of a leaf
Tuber: an enlarged underground stem with many buds called eyes, as in a potato
Umbel: a flower cluster with stems growing from a single point
Whorl: many leaves growing around a stem at the same point

ILLUSTRATED GLOSSARY

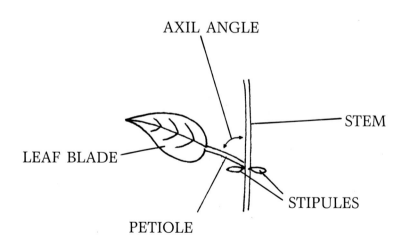

LEAVES

LINEAR   LANCEOLATE   OVATE   HEART-SHAPED   ARROW-SHAPED

LOBED   CLEFT   PINNATE   PALMATE

HOW LEAVES ATTACH TO STEMS

BASAL   OPPOSITE   ALTERNATE

WHORLED   CLASPING   PERFOLIATE

FLOWERS

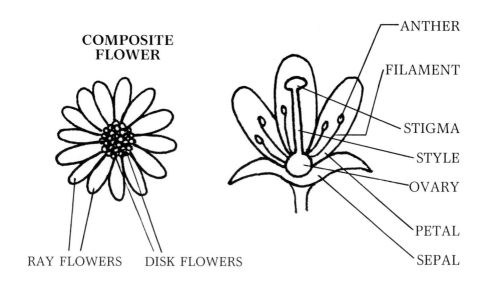

COMPOSITE FLOWER

ANTHER

FILAMENT

STIGMA

STYLE

OVARY

PETAL

SEPAL

RAY FLOWERS   DISK FLOWERS

ANTHER + FILAMENT = STAMEN
STIGMA + STYLE + OVARY = PISTIL
ALL OF THE PETALS = COROLLA
ALL OF THE SEPALS = CALYX

HOW FLOWERS ATTACH TO STEMS

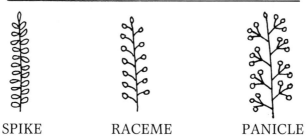

SPIKE   RACEME   PANICLE

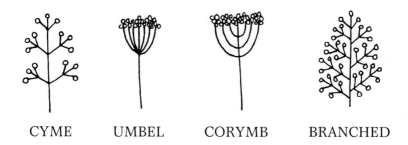

CYME   UMBEL   CORYMB   BRANCHED

PHOTOGRAPHING WILDFLOWERS

FILM
Use high speed film with an ASA of at least 200. For colored slides, Ektachrome emphasizes the cooler tones and Kodachrome and Fujichrome the warmer ones. Ektachrome and Fujichrome can usually be processed overnight at your local photo shop. For colored prints, Kodacolor Gold, Konica, and Ektar (1000 ASA) are also good.

COMPOSITION
When composing your photograph, be sure to check that there are no distractions such as weeds, other plants, colors, etc. in the foreground or background. Sometimes rocks or textures can add interest to your photograph.

FOCUS
If you have one, use a macro lens for close-ups. A 135 or 105 mm "portrait" lens narrows the depth of field (blurs the background), helping the flower that you are trying to photograph stand out more clearly in the foreground. If there is any breeze, a tripod and higher shutter speed sometimes help. There tends to be less wind in the early morning and late afternoon. When pressing the shutter release, hold your camera as still as possible and press down smoothly. No jerking!

LIGHT
Flowers near the ground need more light. If your light meter reads F11 when you are standing up, your aperture should be opened at least one more stop (F8) when closer to the ground. "Bracketing" is taking several photographs of the same subject using different lens openings and different speeds. This helps to assure you of at least one good exposure. Backlighting can also be used effectively. A fill-in flash is helpful if more light is needed.

IDENTIFICATION
As well as taking photographs of different parts of the wildflower, try to include one of the entire plant. Carry a notepad with you to keep track of which flower you have photographed and the ecosystem in which you found it. Did you find it under a lodgepole pine, in a high desert, above the timberline, or in a boggy meadow? Write it down.

EDITING
As soon as your photographs are developed, look at them and THROW AWAY any that are poor compositions, out-of-focus, overexposed, or underexposed. This will save you time, storage space, and friends who otherwise will never look at another photograph you take again!

BLADDER CAMPION
Silene cucubalus
Pink Family

FOUND
- in dry or disturbed places

BLOOMS
- July—August

HEIGHT
- up to 3'

FLOWERS
- 2 lobed white petal in cymes
- calyx is hairy
- at maturity, the calyx forms a globe with reddish-brown veins

STEMS
- downy

LEAVES
- opposite and lanceolate
- more narrow towards the stem
- mainly on lower part of the plant

INTERESTING FACT
- also know as "Catchfly"

LABRADOR TEA
Ledum groenlandicum
Heath Family

FOUND
- boggy places

BLOOMS
- July—August

INDIAN USE
- leaves used for making tea

HEIGHT
- 1—4′ shrub

FLOWERS
- white
- 5 lobed petals
- 5—10 stamen
- grow in a corymb

STEMS
- woody

LEAVES
- alternate
- oblong
- evergreen
- dark color above
- rusty colored and wooly underneath

AMERICAN BISTORT

Polygonum bistortoides
Buckwheat Family

HEIGHT
- 1—2'

FLOWERS
- 1—2" long
- in a ball of small, white flowers, each with 5 petal-like segments
- 8 stamens

STEMS
- slender
- a few small leaves sheathing the stem

LEAVES
- broad and lance-shaped
- basal with stems

ROOT
- thick and twisted

FOUND
- wet, boggy meadows, from valley floors to high mountain meadows

BLOOMS
- June—August

INDIAN USE
- roots roasted, eaten raw, or boiled

WILDLIFE USE
- roots eaten by bears and rodents
- leaves are forage for deer and elk

BUCKWHEAT

Eriogonum sp.
Buckwheat Family

FOUND
- open dry areas, especially with sagebrush

BLOOMS
- May—July

INDIAN USE
- antidote for poison
- treatment for sore throats
- tea made from leaves

WILDLIFE USE
- seeds gathered by rodents

INTERESTING FACT
- many different species have evolved from differing habitats

HEIGHT
- 6—18″

FLOWERS
- cream- to rose-colored as flower matures; one bright yellow variety is called "Sulphur Plant"
- compound umbels of many small flowers
- no petals, 4—6 sepals, 6—9 stamens

STEMS
- growing from a thick clump of leaves that hugs the ground

LEAVES
- lanceolate to linear in shape
- lighter in color underneath
- alternate

GLOBE FLOWER

Trollius laxus
Buttercup Family

HEIGHT
- ½—1½'

FLOWERS
- 5—8 white sepals that resemble petals
- numerous yellow stamens
- dark green ovaries in the center

STEMS
- of different heights growing from the same plant
- each stem usually bears a single flower

LEAVES
- palmate with 5 lobes, deeply notched

FOUND
- boggy streamsides and meadows
- near melting snow

BLOOMS
- May—July

MARSH MARIGOLD

Caltha leptosepala
Buttercup Family

HEIGHT
- 3—6''

FLOWERS
- 1—2'' across
- large, white, buttercup-type flowers
- no petals, many thin white sepals
- numerous yellow stamens
- several pistils

STEMS
- leafless

LEAVES
- large, basal, ovate, dark green, and shiny

FOUND
- streambanks
- wet meadows

BLOOMS
- May—July

INTERESTING FACTS
- somewhat poisonous if eaten in large quantities
- blooms as soon as the snow melts

SHOWY FLEABANE DAISY

Erigeron speciosus
Composite Family

HEIGHT
- 1—2′

FLOWERS
- many purple, pink, or white, thin ray flowers (about 100)
- bracts are the same size and do not overlap

STEMS
- branch near the top to hold many flowers

LEAVES
- lanceolate and somewhat curled
- mid-stem leaves are clasping

FOUND
- moist to dry soils
- open woods and meadows
- aspen groves

BLOOMS
- June—August

INTERESTING FACT
- folklore claims that this plant protects against fleas

MULES' EARS
Wyethia helianthoides √
Composite Family

FOUND
- open, wet,
  mountain meadows

BLOOMS
- May—June

HEIGHT
- 1—3′

FLOWERS
- 2½—5″ across (the
  largest white-
  flowered member of
  Composite Family)
- sometimes yellow
- 1 or more flower
  heads on a stem
- 10—20 white rays
  (some tipped); with
  bright, yellow-orange
  disk flowers in the
  center
- many overlapping,
  hairy bracts

STEMS
- coarse, bunched, and
  hairy
- grow from a woody
  taproot

LEAVES
- can be almost 1′ long
- smaller as they grow
  up stem
- large, shiny, and
  bright green
- alternate and mainly
  basal

INTERESTING FACT
- named for Capt.
  Nathaniel Wyeth
  (1802—1856), the
  Western explorer and
  trader who established
  the first fur-trading
  post (Fort Hall) near
  Pocatello, Idaho

INDIAN USE
- cooked the roots

WILDLIFE USE
- young leaves eaten by
  deer, elk, and bears

PEARLY EVERLASTING
Anaphalis margaritacea
Composite Family

HEIGHT
• 1—3'

FLOWERS
• clusters of white, pearl-shaped flowers that are actually made of bracts, not petals
• tiny disk flowers in the center are yellowish green and tubular

STEMS
• light greyish green and downy
• erect and holding a clustered head of flowers at the top

LEAVES
• narrow and long, 2—5"
• greyish green on top and downy underneath
• lance-shaped

FOUND
• dry roadsides and disturbed areas
• grows in clumps

BLOOMS
• June—August

INTERESTING FACTS
• *margaritacea* means "pearl"
• easily dried for floral arrangements

17

YARROW

Achillea lanulosa
Composite Family

HEIGHT
- 1—3'

FLOWERS
- flat clusters of tiny, white ray flowers
- disk flowers are slightly darker

STEMS
- hairy, fibrous, and very tough

LEAVES
- fern-like, pinnately divided
- soft and lacy, aromatic

FOUND
- dry to moist soil
- widely distributed

BLOOMS
- May—September

INDIAN USE
- leaves were used as a poultice for wounds and also steeped for a medicinal tea

INTERESTING FACT
- flower heads dried for arrangements

PARROT'S BEAK

Pedicularis racemosa
Figwort Family

HEIGHT
- ½—1½'

FLOWERS
- pinkish-white flowers grow loosely on short stems from the axils on a raceme
- 2 large upper petals unite to form a beak which almost touches the lower lip.

STEMS
- tall, erect, and can be reddish in color

LEAVES
- long, lanceolate with tiny notches along the edges

FOUND
- in high altitudes
- moist meadows, conifer woods

BLOOMS
- July—August

INTERESTING FACTS
- *pedicularis* means "louse"
- early farmers thought this plant gave their cattle lice

SYRINGA

Philadelphus lewisii
Hydrangea Family

FOUND
- medium dry to moist soil
- along streamsides and in canyons

BLOOMS
- May—July

INTERESTING FACTS
- also known as "Mock Orange" because of its fragrance
- collected and recorded by Meriwether Lewis during the 1806 Lewis and Clark expedition
- state flower of Idaho

HEIGHT
- 4—8'

FLOWERS
- 4—5 white petals
- many prominent yellow stamens
- grow in clusters

STEMS
- woody and branching

LEAVES
- can be 3" long
- opposite and ovate on short stems
- slightly serrated along edges

INDIAN USE
- arrows fashioned from the straight, sturdy stems

WILDLIFE USE
- forage for deer and elk

COMMON BEAR GRASS

Xerophyllum tenax
Lily Family

HEIGHT
- 3—5'

FLOWERS
- 6—8" torch-like spike of numerous small white flowers
- 6-petaled, each a miniature lily

STEMS
- stout and unbranched
- covered with shorter, needle-like leaves

LEAVES
- basal and numerous
- grass-like, 1—2½' long
- very narrow, stiff, and sharp-edged

FOUND
- open woods
- slopes and clearings

BLOOMS
- June—September
- does not bloom every year, but usually every 5—7 years

INDIAN USE
- leaves used for weaving baskets and clothing

WILDLIFE USE
- flowers are eaten by bears, goats, deer, and elk

MOUNTAIN DEATH CAMAS
Zigadenus elegans
Lily Family

HEIGHT
- 1—2′

FLOWERS
- grow in a spray
- white with a yellowish green, heart-shaped gland near the base
- 6 stamens, 3 sepals, and 3 petals (appears to be 6 petals)

STEMS
- slender

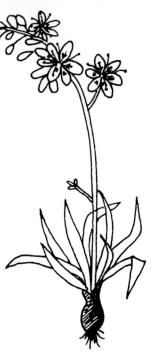

LEAVES
- numerous basal, grass-like leaves

BULB
- blackish on outside

FOUND
- moist meadows
- along streambanks

BLOOMS
- June—August

INTERESTING FACT
- **Contains alkaloids that are extremely poisionous to man and beast!**

WILD ONION

Allium brandegei
Lily Family

HEIGHT
• 2—6″

FLOWERS
• umbel of many small, white flowers
• difficult to differentiate petals and sepals
• combined petals and sepals total 6; 6 stamens
• outer sepals have a greenish midvein
• the 2 bracts under the umbel sometimes drop before the flower blooms

STEMS
• single and growing from a bulb
• shorter than the uppermost leaves

LEAVES
• generally 2 or more
• long and narrow
• grow from an edible bulb

FOUND
• sandy, moist meadows

BLOOMS
• May—July

INDIAN USE
• eaten raw or cooked
• rubbed over bodies as an insect repellent

WILDLIFE USE
• greens and bulbs eaten by ground squirrels, deer, elk, and bears

INTERESTING FACTS
• onions, garlic, chives, shallots, and leeks all belong to this genus
• the Lewis and Clark expedition found this a welcome seasoning to their bland diet

FALSE SOLOMON'S SEAL

Smilacina racemosa
Lily Family

HEIGHT
- 2—3'

FLOWERS
- tiny, white, and in clusters at the top of the plant

STEMS
- arching or erect
- sometimes slightly bent where leaves attach

LEAVES
- large, broad, ovate leaves sometimes clasp the stem
- alternate and ribbed

INTERESTING FACT
- fruit at first is a small, speckled, greenish white berry that becomes red as it ripens

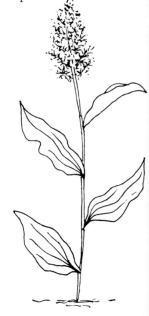

FOUND
- moist, wooded areas
- in dense patches

BLOOMS
- May—July

WILD LILY-OF-THE-VALLEY
Smilacina stellata
Lily Family

HEIGHT
- 1—2'

FLOWERS
- larger than False Solomon's Seal
- widely spaced on a raceme that consists of up to 15 white flowers
- 4 petals (lilies usually have 3 or 6)
- 6 stamens

STEMS
- erect, unbranched, and leafy

LEAVES
- lanceolate and folded in center
- highly visible parallel ribs

FOUND
- moist, mostly shaded wooded areas
- usually found growing with False Solomon's Seal

BLOOMS
- May—July

WILDLIFE USE
- elk and deer eat the young shoots

INTERESTING FACT
- spotted, greenish white berries turn pale red as they ripen

25

SEGO LILY
Calochortus nutallii
Lily Family

INDIAN USE
- bulb cooked, eaten raw, or dried and used for making bread

WILDLIFE USE
- food source for rodents and bears

INTERESTING FACTS
- a staple for early pioneers, especially Mormon immigrants
- state flower of Utah
- greatly prized for its delicious, potato-like flavor and high nutrition

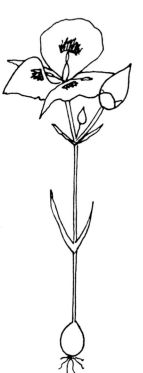

HEIGHT
- 8—15″

FLOWERS
- 3 white petals, 3 white sepals, 3 stamens
- rounded petals with a slight tip in the center of the outer edge
- each petal is marked with a purple spot
- greenish gland with yellow hairs in the center of the corolla

STEMS
- erect, unbranched

LEAVES
- very few
- long, narrow, and grass-like

FOUND
- dry, rocky, and sandy soil
- often among sagebrush and on mountain slopes

BLOOMS
- June—July

BOG ORCHID
Habenaria dilatata
Orchid Family

HEIGHT
• 10—20"

FLOWERS
• white to yellowish green
• spike of many small flowers close to the stem
• fragrant

STEMS
• thick and fleshy

LEAVES
• linear, approximately 6" long
• bright yellow-green
• get smaller as they go upward
• succulent

ROOTS
• tuberous

FOUND
• in full sun or partial shade
• along streambanks
• boggy places

BLOOMS
• June—August

INDIAN USE
• boiled bulbs as a food source

27

COW PARSNIP

Heracleum lanatum
Parsley Family

HEIGHT
- 3—8′

FLOWERS
- 4—6″ across
- creamy white, small flowers in an umbel-like cluster
- have a strong odor

STEMS
- thick and hollow

LEAVES
- extremely large, divided into 3 deeply lobed segments
- sharply toothed

FOUND
- along streambanks and in other moist places

BLOOMS
- May—July

INDIAN USE
- to treat arthritis and rheumatism

WILDLIFE USE
- forage plant for deer, elk, bear, and sheep
- seeds eaten by several species of birds

YAMPAH

Perideridia gairdneri
Parsley Family

HEIGHT
- 1—3′

FLOWERS
- tiny and white
- grow on compound umbels

STEMS
- single, slender
- branching at the top

LEAVES
- slender, linear, and pinnately divided

ROOTS
- large, fleshy taproot
- divided into 2 or 3 segments

FOUND
- open, dry meadows

BLOOMS
- June—August

INDIAN USE
- important food source
- root eaten raw or ground into flour

WILDLIFE USE
- eaten by rodents and bears

INTERESTING FACT
- be very careful in identifying this plant as other related members of the Parsley Family are poisonous!

CHICKWEED
Stellaria jamesiana
Pink Family

HEIGHT
- about 16″

FLOWERS
- 5 petals with deep notch at tip
- 5 sepals
- twice as many stamens as petals

STEMS
- thin, downy, and sticky

LEAVES
- long, linear, and in pairs

FOUND
- woods
- alpine meadows
- dry, rocky slopes

BLOOMS
- May—July

INDIAN USE
- gathered leaves early in season to use in salads
- used to reduce fevers

INTERESTING FACT
- *stellaria* refers to the star-shaped flowers

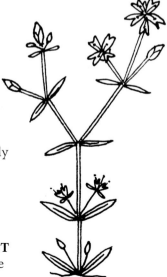

SPRING BEAUTY
Claytonia lanceolata
Purslane Family

HEIGHT
- 2—7″

FLOWERS
- pinkish white and have 5 petals with darker veins
- 2 sepals, 5 bright pink stamens

STEMS
- several, growing from a deep underground tuber

LEAVES
- 2 basal leaves, long, lanceolate, and opposite

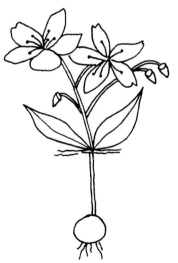

FOUND
- wet areas, as the snow melts
- low-growing

BLOOMS
- April—July

INDIAN USE
- tubers eaten raw or boiled

WILDLIFE USE
- early spring grazing for deer, elk, and sheep

STICKY CINQUEFOIL
Potentilla glandulosa ✓
Rose Family

HEIGHT
- 1—3'

FLOWERS
- white or yellow
- 5 broad petals, 5 sepals, and 5 bracts
- numerous stamens and pistils

STEMS
- hairy and sticky

LEAVES
- strawberry-like leaves
- sharply toothed

FOUND
- many different habitats
- usually in open areas

BLOOMS
- May—July

INDIAN USE
- made tea from leave for a mouthwash
- poultice for wounds

INTERESTING FACT
- *cinquefoil* means "fiv leaves"
- differs from Buttercu in having 5 bracts
- many different speci of cinquefoil are fou: in the Rocky Mountain area

LACY DAISY

Matricaria inodora
Composite Family

FOUND
- in abundance in high altitudes
- on dry hillsides and open areas

BLOOMS
- late July through September

INTERESTING FACTS
- a scentless chamomile
- a variety of *Matricaria maritima*

HEIGHT
- 2—3′

FLOWERS
- numerous white daisies with ray and disc flowers occuring on the ends of branches
- seeds are elongated pods with vertical lines

STEMS
- numerous and branching

LEAVES
- occur alternately and are pinnately divided
- are lacy and fernlike

INDIAN USE
- leaves from plants of this species are used to make a calming tea for stomachs and nerves

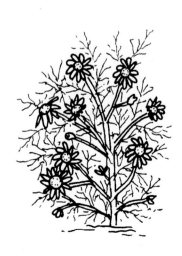

SAXIFRAGE

Saxifraga sp.
Saxifrage Family

HEIGHT
- ½—1'

FLOWERS
- regular and delicate
- colors vary from white to yellow to pink
- 5 spreading petals, 5—10 stamens

STEMS
- straight, erect, and almost leafless

LEAVES
- basal and alternate

FOUND
- along edges of springs and streams, usually in shaded areas

BLOOMS
- July—August

Brook Saxifrage *(Saxifraga arguta)* and Grass of Parnassus *(Parnassia fimbriata)* are usually found growing together as pictured above. See close-up photo and drawing of Brook Saxifrage on opposite page. Grass of Parnassus closely resembles One-flowered Wintergreen. Look for smooth, kidney-shaped basal leaves and upright flower heads with yellow-green styles on Grass of Parnassus.

ONE-FLOWERED WINTERGREEN
Moneses uniflora
Wintergreen Family

FLOWERS
- 5 white, frilly petals
- 10 yellow-green stamens
- long, green style
- slight fragrance

STEMS
- leafless and bent near the top

LEAVES
- small, round and basal
- slightly notched around margins

FOUND
- shady, mossy areas under conifers

BLOOMS
- July—August

INTERESTING FACT
- also known as "Wood Nymph"

BROOK SAXIFRAGE
Saxifraga arguta

VALERIAN
Valeriana sitchensis
Valerian Family

HEIGHT
- 1—4'

FLOWERS
- pale lavender buds turn white as flower matures
- grow in clusters
- 5 petals
- 3 stamens and long pistils extend beyond the tube-shaped corolla

STEMS
- somewhat succulent

LEAVES
- mostly basal, opposite
- often pinnately divided

FOUND
- moist places and open woods

BLOOMS
- June—August

WILDLIFE USE
- deer, elk, and other big game eat the leaves and stems
- attracts insects

INTERESTING FACTS
- also known as "Wild Heliotrope"
- some species used for medicinal purposes

ELKWEED - GREEN GENTIAN - MONUMENT PLANT

Frasera speciosa
Gentian Family

HEIGHT
- 2—5'

FLOWERS
- numerous greenish white flowers, spotted with purple
- 4 petals with pointed lobes, 4 stamens, 4 narrow bracts
- pinkish hairs around the nectar gland at the base of each petal
- green ovary in the center rests on top of the corolla

STEMS
- a single, thick, unbranched stem holds erect a large cone-shaped plant
- flower stems grow from the axil where leaves join the main stem

LEAVES
- lance-shaped and whorled around the main stem of the plant
- very large at the base, diminishing in size as they grow up the stem

FOUND
- open areas
- dry to moist soil

BLOOMS
- June—July
- biennial (the first year it is a cluster of leaves)

WILDLIFE USE
- leaves provide forage for deer, elk, and cattle

INTERESTING FACT
- can go for many years without blooming, storing energy in its taproot

37

PINESAP
Monotropa hypopitys
Heath Family

HEIGHT
- ½—1′

FLOWERS
- tawny to cream-colored
- on a raceme, nodding and bell-shaped
- 4—5 petals and sepals
- twice as many stamens

STEM
- nodding and very fragile

LEAVES
- no real leaves, but small scales grow up the stem

FOUND
- damp humus of shady coniferous forests

BLOOMS
- June—August

INTERESTING FACTS
- a saprophyte, it lacks chlorophyll, and lives on decaying organic material
- difficult to find

FALSE HELLEBORE
Veratrum viride
Lily Family

HEIGHT
• 3—6'

FLOWERS
• greenish yellow, ½''
  across
• dense clusters on
  many branches that
  start to droop as
  they near the top of
  this large plant
• 6 star-shaped petals
• have a strong odor

STEMS
• single, tall, and
  sturdy

LEAVES
• numerous and up to
  a foot in length with
  highly visible ribs
• overlap each other
  as they grow up the
  stem

FOUND
• wet thickets and
  open mountain
  valleys
• grows in thick
  patches

BLOOMS
• June—July

INDIAN USE
• to lower blood
  pressure
• to cure headaches

INTERESTING FACTS
• most grazing animals
  will avoid this plant
• can be fatal if young
  shoots are eaten,
  because of high
  alkaloid content
• flowers fatal to
  insects
• can be devastating to
  honey bees

PYROLA
Pyrola secunda
Wintergreen Family

HEIGHT
- 2–8″

FLOWERS
- very small, whitish green, growing on one side of a bent raceme
- 5 petals, 10 stamens
- noticeable style protrudes from the corolla, which hangs facing downward from the stem

STEMS
- bent and almost leafless

LEAVES
- basal, ovate, evergreen, shiny, and slightly scalloped

FOUND
- in dry or moist, deep woods

BLOOMS
- July—September

INTERESTING FACT
- also known as "One-sided Wintergreen"

WAYSIDE GROMWELL
Lithospermum ruderale
Borage Family

HEIGHT
- 10—20''

FLOWERS
- tiny, pale yellow flowers
- growing from the axils of the upper leaves
- tube-shaped corolla opens into 5 petals

STEMS
- many and unbranched
- hairy and rough to the touch

LEAVES
- numerous and linear
- can be up to 4'' long
- deeply incised center vein

ROOTS
- woody taproot

FOUND
- open dry places, hillsides, and roadsides

BLOOMS
- May—July

INDIAN USE
- as a source for food and medicine
- roots valued for purple dye

BUTTER AND EGGS

Linaria vulgaris
Figwort Family

FOUND
- roadsides and disturbed areas
- many plants at one site

BLOOMS
- July—September

INDIAN USE
- tea made from leaves used for constipation
- salve for insect bites
- throat ailments
- dye

INTERESTING FACTS
- introduced from Eurasia
- now considered a pesty weed

HEIGHT
- 1—2'

FLOWERS
- ½—1½'' long
- light to bright yellow with a yellow-orange patch at the throat
- resemble snapdragons
- 5 petals: 2 upper lobes point forward, 3 lower lobes bend backwards
- the long corolla is spurred at its base

STEMS
- upright
- many small, linear leaves along the stem

LEAVES
- greyish green and narrow
- alternate and stemless

ROOTS
- creeping

BLAZING STAR
Mentzelia laevicaulis
Loasaceae Family

FOUND
- dry, sandy soils on hillsides and in valleys

BLOOMS
- late June—August

INTERESTING FACTS
- also called "Sand Lily" and "Stickleaf"

HEIGHT
- 1—3'

FLOWERS
- lemon yellow
- 2—4" across
- grow at the end of branches
- 5 petals are pointed
- underneath are a few toothed bracts which are long and narrow
- numerous showy stamen

STEMS
- smooth

LEAVES
- grow up to 6" long
- are broadly lanceolate and barbed
- are alternate except on flowering branches where they are opposite

INDIAN USE
- seeds are dried and ground

INTERESTING FACTS
- barbs on the leaves often attach themselves to clothing

GOLDENROD ✓

Solidago elongata
Composite Family

LEAVES
- alternate and thin
- lanceolate
- usually 2—5″ long
- smooth or toothed

FOUND
- along roadsides and open disturbed areas
- usually found growing together in a group of several plants

BLOOMS
- July—September

HEIGHT
- 1—3′

FLOWERS
- yellow, dense panicle heads
- composite flowers

STEMS
- branching

INTERESTING FACTS
- about 100 different species
- some species have flowers on just one side of curved branch
- heralds the end of summer
- usually grows in small groups

FIDDLENECK
Amsinckia menziesii
Borage Family

HEIGHT
- 1—2'

FLOWERS
- orangish yellow on a coiled cyme
- 5-petaled, small-tubed corolla surrounding stamens

STEMS
- very bristly and coiled at the top

LEAVES
- lanceolate and bristly

FOUND
- dry open fields, along roads

BLOOMS
- May—July

ALPINE BUTTERCUP

Ranunculus adoneus
Buttercup Family

INDIAN USE
- roasted seeds that were then ground into flour for bread
- yellow petals used as a dye

WILDLIFE USE
- food source for pikas and other animals
- seeds eaten by rodents

INTERESTING FACTS
- can cause skin irritation if handled
- most are toxic if eaten

HEIGHT
- 4—10''

FLOWERS
- ½—1'' wide
- 5 or more bright yellow and waxy petals

STEMS
- clustered together at the base

LEAVES
- 3—5 segments
- deeply toothed

FOUND
- high elevations
- wet areas

BLOOMS
- July—August

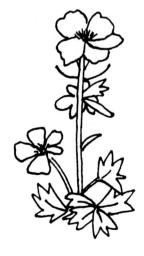

HEART-LEAF ARNICA

Arnica cordifolia
Composite Family

HEIGHT
• 1½—2½'

FLOWERS
• 10—14 ray flowers
• heads approximately 2½" across
• petals and centers are the same yellow color
• bracts have long hairs

STEMS
• hairy

LEAVES
• 1½—5" long
• heart-shaped
• serrated edges
• opposite and paired
• long stalks at base, getting shorter as they go up stem

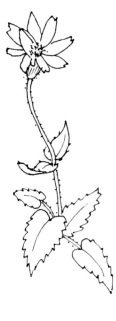

FOUND
• partial shade
• open lodgepole pine and Douglas fir forests

BLOOMS
• June—September

INDIAN USE
• stems used on cuts to prevent infection and reduce swelling

INTERESTING FACT
• **POISONOUS IF EATEN**

ARROWLEAF BALSAMROOT
Balsamorhiza sagittata
Composite Family

HEIGHT
- 1—2'

FLOWERS
- 4—5'' across
- bright yellow flower heads
- bracts very hairy
- strong smelling

STEMS
- almost leafless

LEAVES
- basal, heart-shaped
- silvery gray-green because of numerous fine hairs
- smooth outer margins

FOUND
- in sunny areas, dry hills, and open pine forests
- in clumps of many flowers

BLOOMS
- May—June

INDIAN USE
- boiled or roasted stems, roots, and seeds
- leaves were eaten raw in salad
- aromatic sap used for coughs
- roots for rheumatism, headaches, and insect bites

WILDLIFE USE
- important forage for sheep, deer, and elk

FALSE (OR MOUNTAIN) DANDELION

Agoseris glauca
Composite Family

FOUND
- dry to wet soil
- meadows and mountain slopes

BLOOMS
- May—August

HEIGHT
- ½—2'

FLOWERS
- yellow color more dull than common dandelion
- ray flowers in the middle with shorter petals
- ends of petals finely toothed

STEMS
- leafless

LEAVES
- lanceolate and toothed, in a basal rosette

SEEDS
- ball of white, finely haired, parachute-type seeds
- easily distributed by wind

INDIAN USE
- the rubbery juice of stems and leaves was dried and used for gum

WILDLIFE USE
- many animals graze upon this plant

INTERESTING FACT
- leaves and stems have milky sap

SHRUBBY GOLDENWEED

Haplopappus suffruticosus
Composite Family

HEIGHT
- 1—2′

FLOWERS
- heads are often single
- usually 3—8 yellow rays
- parts of the disk flowers are long and delicate

STEMS
- woody shrub

LEAVES
- hairy and fragrant
- mostly basal and alternate

ROOTS
- deep taproot

FOUND
- dry, rocky soil

BLOOMS
- July—August

GROUNDSEL

Senecio triangularis
Composite Family

HEIGHT
- 2—4′

FLOWERS
- numerous disk flowers are compact and orange-yellow
- heads are in a cluster
- flattened on top
- 6—12 yellow ray petals
- involucre of bracts are even and do not overlap

STEMS
- single and erect, branching at the top

LEAVES
- 2—7″ long
- alternate, triangular and sharply toothed
- leaf stalk joins the main stem angling slightly upward

FOUND
- along stream banks and in other wet areas
- other species may be found in drier, more sandy places

BLOOMS
- July—September

WILDLIFE USE
- because of alkaloid content, sometimes fatal to cattle and horses if eaten in large amounts

INTERESTING FACTS
- this genus is among the largest of flowering plants
- seeds are covered with white hairs

SALSIFY

Tragopogon dubius
Composite Family

FOUND
- dry, disturbed areas, fields, waste places

BLOOMS
- June—August

INTERESTING FACTS
- imported from Europe and brought to the West by early settlers
- also known as "Goatsbeard" or "Oyster Plant" (early settlers thought the taproot tasted like oysters)
- showy seedhead is widely used in dried arrangements

HEIGHT
- 1—4"

FLOWERS
- many rayed, yellow
- several long, narrow, radiating green bracts extend beyond the petals
- center disk flowers are the same color yellow, and have dark flecks
- individual seeds are longer, with attached parachute darker, less compact, than that of the "False Dandelion"

STEMS
- erect, support a single flower
- contain a white, milky juice

LEAVES
- numerous, alternate, and grass-like
- clasp the stem

ROOTS
- taproots are biennial

EVENING PRIMROSE

Oenothera heterantha
Evening Primrose Family

HEIGHT
- 2—5"

FLOWERS
- bright yellow, growing in the center of a rosette of leaves
- 4 petals, 4 sepals, 4—8 stamens

STEMS
- practially non-existent

LEAVES
- smooth, mostly basal, and whorled
- on very short stems with a noticeable reddish midrib

ROOT
- taproot

FOUND
- growing low to the ground
- in damp meadows and along streamsides

BLOOMS
- May—July

WILDLIFE USE
- in some species, seeds are eaten by birds and small animals

INTERESTING FACT
- flowers open in the evening and are pollinated by insects that are active during the night

MONKEY-FLOWER

Mimulus sp.
Figwort Family

YELLOW MONKEY-FLOWER

Mimulus guttatus

HEIGHT
- ½—3'

FLOWERS
- have stems and grow from axils
- irregular and look like a snapdragon
- yellow to red to purple in color
- 5 petals joined to form a corolla; upper 2 lobes bend upward, lower 3 lobes bend downward
- 4 stamens
- some species may have spotted and hairy throats

STEMS
- several

LEAVES
- opposite and stalkless
- lanceolate or ovate
- in some species are deeply ribbed or finely toothed

LEWIS MONKEY-FLOWER

Mimulus lewisii

FOUND
- usually in wet places

BLOOMS
- May—July

INDIAN USE
- leaves used for salad greens

WILDLIFE USE
- food source for rodents and hummingbirds during the summer

MULLEIN
Verbascum thapsus
Figwort Family

FOUND
- dry, sandy soils
- roadsides and other disturbed areas

BLOOMS
- June—August

INDIAN USE
- for skin lotion
- to reduce skin inflamation

WILDLIFE USE
- seeds a food source for small birds
- forage for deer and elk during the winter

INTERESTING FACTS
- introduced from Eurasia
- plant is biennial
  1st year: a rosette of leaves
  2nd year: a large stalk of yellow flowers
  3rd year: dead plant turns brown and remains standing

2nd year spike

HEIGHT
- 2—7 '

FLOWERS
- 1/2—1'' across
- bloom sporadically along a dense spike
- 5 petals, 5 stamens

STEMS
- tall, stout, erect and hairy

LEAVES
- grey-green with soft, velvet-like hairs
- ovate and very large (can grow up to almost 1 1/2 ' in length)

1st year rosette

55

GLACIER LILY
Erythronium grandiflorum
Lily Family

INDIAN USE
- boiled or dried for food use during the winter months

WILDLIFE USE
- bulbs and green pods eaten by deer, elk, bighorn sheep, and bears
- rodents dig up this bulb and store it for winter

INTERESTING FACTS
- this plant is also known as "Dogtooth Violet," "Fawn Lily," "Adder's-Tongue," and "Trout Lily"

HEIGHT
- ½—1'

FLOWERS
- bright yellow and drooping
- 3 petals and 3 sepals pointed upwards
- 6 stamens hang below

STEMS
- leafless and curved at the top

LEAVES
- only 2, which are broad, basal, pointed, and shiny

ROOTS
- bulbs

FOUND
- rich, moist soil along streambanks, in meadows and woods
- found in Yellowstone National Park in great profusion

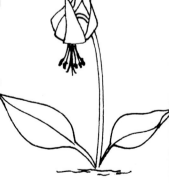

BLOOMS
- May—June
- just after the snow melts

SHRUBBY CINQUEFOIL

Potentilla fruticosa
Rose Family

HEIGHT
- 1—4'

FLOWERS
- yellow, about 1" across
- 5 petals, 5 sepals, many stamens

STEMS
- many branched, woody, and shrubby
- reddish brown bark can be easily stripped

LEAVES
- greyish green, small, leathery leaflets

FOUND
- near water sources
- open forests
- from plains to high elevations

BLOOMS
- June—August

INDIAN USE
- made tea from leaves

WILDLIFE USE
- plant retains its leaves during the winter months, which provides forage for large animals

INTERESTING FACTS
- used as an ornamental shrub in high altitude gardens
- *fruticosa* means "shrubby"

STONECROP
Sedum lanceolatum
Stonecrop Family

HEIGHT
- 4—8''

FLOWERS
- yellow and sometimes tinged with purple
- in dense clusters (cymes)
- 5 petals, 8—10 long, yellow stamens

STEMS
- short and reddish

LEAVES
- single, alternate, short, and fleshy
- pale green to reddish

FOUND
- dry, rocky places
- growing in small clumps

BLOOMS
- June—August

INTERESTING FACTS
- a succulent, it stores water in its stems and leaves
- can remain dormant for long periods during droughts

GOOSEFOOT VIOLET

Viola purpurea
Violet Family

HEIGHT
- 2—6″

FLOWERS
- 5 bright yellow petals, sometimes with purplish tinge on the back
- 2 upper, 2 side, and 1 lower flat petal on which insects land
- dark lines on lower petals, near the throat

STEMS
- slender, clustered, and growing from leaf axils

LEAVES
- lanceolate to rounded and up to 2″ long
- shape of the leaves gives this plant its name
- prominent veins incised on the top of the leaf become ridges underneath

FOUND
- moist, shady areas

BLOOMS
- May—August

INDIAN USE
- salad greens

SITKA COLUMBINE
Aquilegia formosa
Buttercup Family

HEIGHT
- 1—3'

FLOWERS
- 5 yellow petals with reddish spurs that bend backward
- 5 reddish sepals
- 5 yellow pistils and many yellow stamens

STEMS
- long and drooping

LEAVES
- mostly basal with long stems
- deeply lobed

FOUND
- wet woodlands and canyon banks

BLOOMS
- June—August

WILDLIFE USE
- hummingbirds and butterflies, attracted to the bright color, feed on nectar

INTERESTING FACT
- *formosa* means "beautiful"

LEOPARD LILY

Fritillaria atropurpurea
Lily Family

HEIGHT
- ½—2'

FLOWERS
- yellowish green petals mottled with brownish purple on the inside
- outsides of petals light brown with brown to purple speckles
- prominent orange-yellow stamens
- 1—4 drooping flowers on each stem

STEMS
- slender and unbranched

LEAVES
- narrow, long, and linear
- greyish green

FOUND
- rich, moist soil in mountain valleys
- damp woods

BLOOMS
- May—June

INDIAN USE
- starchy corms are a food source

INTERESTING FACTS
- strong odor attracts insects
- difficult to find

61

SORREL - DOCK
Rumex sp.
Buckwheat Family

HEIGHT
- 1—3'

FLOWERS
- green when first blooming, turning reddish with age
- 6 sepals in 2 circles

STEMS
- tall and erect

LEAVES
- long, lanceolate

FOUND
- fields and roadsides

BLOOMS
- May—July

INDIAN USE
- roots used for dyes

INTERESTING FACT
- imported from Eurasia

ORANGE GLOBE MALLOW
Sphaeralcea munroana
Mallow Family

HEIGHT
- ½—2′

FLOWERS
- in clusters, light orange to red in color
- 5 petals that form a cup-shaped flower
- stamens joined together around the pistil

STEMS
- tough and hairy

LEAVES
- greyish green in color
- equally broad and long, toothed

FOUND
- dry, sandy soil

BLOOMS
- June—August

WILDLIFE USE
- grazing for deer and sheep

SPOTTED CORALROOT
Corallorhiza maculata
Orchid Family

HEIGHT
- ½—2'

FLOWERS
- reddish brown
- many on a raceme
- lower white lip is spotted with crimson

STEMS
- reddish brown in color
- several bracts but no leaves

FOUND
- moist woods, amid decaying organic matter

BLOOMS
- June—July

INTERESTING FACTS
- a saprophyte, it has no leaves and lacks chlorophyll
- "Striped Coralroot" is a related species

WILD PEONY
Paeonia brownii
Peony Family

HEIGHT
- ½—2'

FLOWERS
- 5—6 light green
  cup-shaped sepals
  surrounding several
  rust-red petals
  tinged with light
  green
- many stamens
  surround 2—5
  pistils that become
  large pods
  containing many
  seeds

STEMS
- several curved
  stems, each holding
  a single flower

LEAVES
- stalks are alternate,
  divided into 3
  segments, each
  deeply cleft

FOUND
- sagebrush country
  and open forests

BLOOMS
- May—June

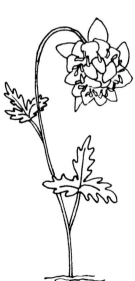

INDIAN PAINTBRUSH ✓

Castilleja sp.
Figwort Family

FOUND
- moist to damp meadows

BLOOMS
- June—August

INTERESTING FACTS
- most species are semi-parasitic
- root system penetrates roots of other plants and saps them of their nourishment
- also known as "Painted-Cup"
- very difficult to identify the different red species
- in most species, plants are covered with very fine hairs

HEIGHT
- ½—2'

FLOWERS
- a small, greenish flower in the center of the top of the plant is almost hidden by the colorful yellow, red, or pink bracts that surround it

STEMS
- mostly single, unbranched, dense spikes growing from a woody root

LEAVES
- leaves (like the bracts) are narrow

OTHER INDIAN PAINTBRUSHES

Castilleja sulphurea

Castilleja rhexifolia

SCARLET GILIA

Gilia aggregata
Phlox Family

FOUND
• dry soils on hillsides
  and along roadsides

BLOOMS
• June—July

HEIGHT
• 1—3′

FLOWERS
• grow in small
  clusters
• long, tubular
  corollas, which are
  brilliant red
• 5 petals, with
  pointed tips
• dainty green bracts
  that curl backwards

STEMS
• usually covered with
  fine hairs

LEAVES
• pinnately divided
  and mostly occurring
  near the base of the
  stem
• crushed leaves emit
  an unpleasant odor

WILDLIFE USE
• hummingbirds collect
  nectar and distribute
  pollen

INTERESTING FACTS
• biennial
• also known as
  "Skyrocket"

MOUNTAIN HEATHER

Phyllodoce empetriformis
Heath Family

HEIGHT
- ½—1½'

FLOWERS
- deep pink, bell-shaped
- 5-lobed corolla
- sepals slightly darker
- stamens almost hidden, but pistil protrudes
- pleasant fragrance

STEMS
- many branched and low-growing
- nodding flowers grow from short, reddish stems

LEAVES
- numerous, small (about ½'' long), and needle-like

FOUND
- low, evergreen shrub
- found in high damp areas, especially around mountain lakes

BLOOMS
- July—August

INTERESTING FACTS
- usually found growing near Alpine Laurel
- Alpine Laurel has a more open flower, and a more rounded leaf

SPIREA - BRIDAL WREATH - MEADOW SWEET
Spirea splendens
Rose Family

HEIGHT
- 2—6'

FLOWERS
- tiny, rose-colored, dense clusters atop a branched stem
- 5 petals, 5 pistils, many stamens

STEMS
- many-branched shrub

LEAVES
- approximately 1'' in length
- ovate with serrated edges

FOUND
- along mountain trails in moist soil, along streams

BLOOMS
- June—August

INDIAN USE
- teas made from stems and leaves

FIREWEED

Epilobium angustifolium
Evening Primrose Family

HEIGHT
- 2—6'

FLOWERS
- dark pink, 4-petaled flowers on a tall spike
- flowers open from the base of the spike
- the new buds droop at the top
- a long pod encases seeds producing long, silky hairs that are widely distributed by wind

STEMS
- tall, erect, and unbranched

LEAVES
- up to 6'' long
- lighter colored underneath
- lanceolate and alternate

FOUND
- sunny, moist places along streams
- open woods and disturbed areas

BLOOMS
- July—August

INDIAN USE
- tea made from dried leaves
- young shoots and leaves used as pot herbs

WILDLIFE USE
- forage for wild animals (a favorite with bears) and livestock

INTERESTING FACTS
- one of the first plants to grow after a forest fire
- helps to control erosion
- also known as "Willow-Herb," since the leaves resemble willow leaves

71

WILD ROSE
Rosa woodsii
Rose Family

HEIGHT
- 3—6' shrub

FLOWERS
- pink with 5 petals, 5 sepals, and many pistils and stamens
- hips turn red and contain many seeds
- very fragrant

STEMS
- branched and thorny

LEAVES
- 2—3 opposite pairs on a stem with 1 single leaf at the tip
- finely serrated edges

FOUND
- in moist soils along streambanks and on hillsides

BLOOMS
- May—July

INDIAN USE
- rose hips used as a food source

WILDLIFE USE
- rose hips are an important winter food for upland game birds and for bears in the fall

INTERESTING FACT
- early settlers made jelly and soups from the hips
- rich in Vitamin C

MOUNTAIN HOLLYHOCK

Iliamna rivularis
Mallow Family

HEIGHT
- 3—6'

FLOWERS
- 1 -2" across and growing on a spike
- pink to lavender petals
- 5 petals form a cup-shaped flower that contains many stamens
- seeds grow in a hairy pouch and are joined together like segments of an orange

STEMS
- sturdy, fibrous, and hairy

LEAVES
- maple shaped with 3—7 lobes
- very large and somewhat crinkly
- covered with tiny hairs

FOUND
- sunny roadsides and open areas

BLOOMS
- June—August

INDIAN USE
- chewed the stems like gum

INTERESTING FACTS
- also known as "Checkermallow"
- *mallow* means "soft" and describes the soft leaves

PRAIRIE SMOKE

Geum triflorum
Rose Family

HEIGHT
- ½—2'

FLOWERS
- nodding and bell-shaped
- 5 rose-colored petals, and 5 narrow bracts that curve outward
- after fertilization, flowers become erect
- feathery plumes grow from the pistils and are easily dispersed by wind and passing animals

STEMS
- droop until the flower is fertilized, then become straight

LEAVES
- mostly basal, fern-like, and with many segments

INDIAN USE
- roots made into a beverage that was also used as an eyewash

INTERESTING FACT
- entire plant is covered with fine down

FOUND
- moist, open areas

BLOOMS
- May—July

STICKY GERANIUM
Geranium viscosissimum
Geranium Family

HEIGHT
- 1–3'

FLOWERS
- 1" across,
  dark pink,
  with distinctive
  purple veins
- 5 petals, 5 sepals,
  10 stamens

STEMS
- branching and
  covered with sticky
  hairs

LEAVES
- covered with sticky
  hairs
- palmately shaped
  into 5–7 segments,
  each deeply cleft

FOUND
- damp to medium-
  dry soil
- aspen groves,
  streamsides, and
  hillsides

BLOOMS
- May–August

WILDLIFE USE
- food source for deer,
  elk, and bears

INTERESTING FACT
- also known as
  "Crane's Bill"
  because of the shape
  of its style

LONG-LEAVED PHLOX

Phlox longifolia
Phlox Family

HEIGHT
- ½—1½′

FLOWERS
- a profusion of flowers growing in loose, flat clusters (cymes)
- color varies from white to pink to lavender
- tube-shaped corolla with 5 petals, symmetrical and spreading

STEMS
- slender and growing in clumps
- more upright than spreading

LEAVES
- opposite, narrow, and linear
- much longer than in other phlox species
- smooth margins

FOUND
- dry, rocky areas

BLOOMS
- May—July

TWEEDYI

Chionophila tweedyi
Figwort Family

HEIGHT
- 2—6″

FLOWERS
- pinkish lavender
- all on one side of a raceme
- long, tubular corolla with 2 lips
- 4 stamens form pollen

STEMS
- comparatively tall, slender, and leafless

LEAVES
- basal, small, and linear

FOUND
- alpine meadows
- near the timberline

BLOOMS
- June—August

INTERESTING FACT
- also known as the "Toothbrush Plant"

MEADOW RUE

Thalictrum occidentale
Buttercup Family

MALE   FEMALE

HEIGHT
- 1—4'

FLOWERS
- have no petals
- bracts on both plants noticeably light in color
- MALE PLANT: greenish purple stamens with yellow tips; in clusters, drooping
- FEMALE PLANT: 10—15 delicate purplish pistils, spread open

STEMS
- very slender, with leaf and flower stems branching out from main stem

LEAVES
- most spectacular part of the plant
- divided into notched segments
- resemble those of a columbine

FOUND
- aspen groves and moist, wooded areas

BLOOMS
- May—July

INDIAN USE
- leaves and seeds valued for their fragrance
- sometimes used as an insect repellent
- roots used as a yellow dye

INTERESTING FACT
- plants are either male or female

GIANT HYSSOP - HORSE MINT

Agastache urticifolia
Mint Family

HEIGHT
- 1—3′

FLOWERS
- white to rose in color
- thick spike at top of stem
- 4 stamens that are longer than petals
- upper lip has 2 lobes

STEMS
- square, as in all members of the Mint Family

LEAVES
- opposite, with a strong aroma of mint
- ovate and toothed

ROOTS
- branching and creeping

FOUND
- moist soil, open valleys, and hillsides

BLOOMS
- June—August

BITTERROOT

Lewisia rediviva
Purslane Family

HEIGHT
- 1—4″
- hugs the ground

FLOWERS
- color varies from white to pink
- large and very showy
- bloom after the leaves wither
- 2—3″ wide
- 12—18 petals
- 6—8 sepals
- 30—50 stamens

STEMS
- several and short
- growing from a root crown

LEAVES
- rise from the root stalk soon after the snow melts
- narrow and succulent, arranged in a rosette

FOUND
- only in sunny areas
- barren, dry, rocky soil, and also on lava flats

BLOOMS
- April—July

INDIAN USE
- roots baked or boiled

INTERESTING FACTS
- species named after Meriwether Lewis of the Lewis and Clark expedition
- can rejuvenate after long droughts
- state flower of Montana

WOODLAND STAR

Lithophragma parviflora
Saxifrage Family

HEIGHT
- 8—20''

FLOWERS
- 3—6, loosely growing on a raceme
- pinkish white, and up to ½'' across
- 5 deeply cleft petals, 5 sepals, 5 stamens

STEMS
- slender, unbranched, and reddish

LEAVES
- mostly basal, small, roundish, and deeply cleft into 3—5 lobes

FOUND
- sagebrush prairies and open forests

BLOOMS
- May—July

WILDLIFE USE
- rodents eat small bulbs

INTERESTING FACTS
- also known as ''Prairie Star'' or ''Starflower''
- small bulbs growing in the leaf axils can become plants

EDULIS
Valeriana edulis
Valerian Family

FOUND
- open, wet places

BLOOMS
- June—July

HEIGHT
- ½—3'

FLOWERS
- tiny, whitish pink flowers clustered into racemes
- have stamens, pistils or both

STEMS
- very thick

LEAVES
- narrow and pinnately divided
- become smaller as they approach the racemes

ROOTS
- thick
- have a strong odor

INDIAN USE
- roots roasted and eaten

WILDLIFE USE
- stems and leaves eaten by larger animals and domestic sheep

INTERESTING FACTS
- *edulis* means "edible"

PUSSYTOES

Antennaria rosea
Composite Family

FOUND
- in high desert prairies
- in mostly dry soils

BLOOMS
- May—August

HEIGHT
- up to 12″

FLOWERS
- pearly white to rose colored
- grow in a cluster at the ends of stems
- are bracts, not petals, and are usually 1/8 to 1/4″ in diameter

STEMS
- are greyish and hairy

LEAVES
- are also greyish and wooly
- are alternate along the stem
- grow in rosettes at the base of the plant

INDIAN USE
- in some species, stems were chewed like a gum

INTERESTING FACTS
- also called "Pink Everlasting" because flowers can be dried

MOUNTAIN PHACELIA
Phacelia sericea
Waterleaf Family

HEIGHT
• up to 1' tall

FLOWERS
• purple in color
• grow on a spike
• 5 stamen protrude from each flower

FOUND
• high altitudes

BLOOMS
• July—August

INTERESTING FACTS
• plant has a fuzzy, feathery look

STEMS
• long and straight

LEAVES
• alternate
• silky and downy
• pinnately divided

THICKSTEM DAISY
Erigeron sp.
Composite Family

Daisies are the largest species of the Composite Family.
They are very difficult to identify and are often confused with asters.
Below is a description of what is commonly called a "Thickstem Daisy."

HEIGHT
- 1—2′

FLOWERS
- 1—2″ across
- many white, pink, or lavender ray flowers
- numerous yellow to orange disk flowers in the center
- small, even bracts (not overlapping) surround the ray flowers

STEMS
- thick, with one flower on a single stem

LEAVES
- mostly basal and lanceolate
- a few small leaves clasp the stems

FOUND
- dry to moist soils
- open woods and meadows

BLOOMS
- May—July

THICKSTEM ASTER

Aster integrifolius
Composite Family

FOUND
• dry meadows and
  open woods

BLOOMS
• late summer
• July—September

HEIGHT
• 1—2'

FLOWERS
• 1—2'' across
• 20 or fewer lavender-
  blue to white ray
  flowers
• disk flowers are
  yellow or orange
• bracts are slightly
  hairy and overlap

STEMS
• comparatively
  thick, tall, and
  slightly hairy

LEAVES
• basal ones are
  broadly lanceolate,
  growing on stems
• midstem leaves
  are single and
  clasping

JACOB'S LADDER
Polemonium pulcherrimum
Phlox Family

HEIGHT
- 1—3'

FLOWERS
- blue-violet
- throat is yellow with several white stamens
- grow in loose clusters along a spike
- 5 petals

STEMS
- grow in clusters
- branched at the top

LEAVES
- pinnately divided
- look like rungs of ladders

ROOT
- a taproot

FOUND
- grassy, moist soil
- along streams and in meadows

BLOOMS
- June—August

INTERESTING FACTS
- related to "Sky Pilot" or "Skunkweed," which are sticky varieties
- leaves of "Sky Pilot" emit a powerful odor when stepped upon

WILD FLAX

Linum lewisii
Flax Family

HEIGHT
- 1—3'

FLOWERS
- 5 blue-lavender petals about 1'' across
- yellow throat with white stamens
- flowers fall off easily when touched
- blossoms close in late afternoon

STEMS
- very thin and sway easily

LEAVES
- many very narrow, ½—1'' long, climb up the stem

FOUND
- dry soil along roadsides
- dry plains and hillsides
- often found with high desert sagebrush

BLOOMS
- June—August

INDIAN USE
- made cordage for many uses, especially fishing tackle

INTERESTING FACT
- used from ancient times for cordage, thread, clothing, and linseed oil

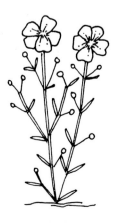

SHOOTING STAR

Dodecatheon pauciflorum
Primrose Family

HEIGHT
- ½—2'

FLOWERS
- 4—5 narrow petals aiming skyward are magenta with white bases
- very dark stamens are fused together to form a beak that points downward

STEMS
- bare, erect, and unbranched

LEAVES
- simple, basal, and more narrow where they join the stem

FOUND
- wet places
- boggy meadows
- streamsides

BLOOMS
- May—July

WILDLIFE USE
- early spring forage for deer and elk

ELEPHANT HEADS

Pedicularis groenlandica
Figwort Family

FOUND
- in very boggy meadows and along streamsides
- in large clusters

BLOOMS
- June—August

HEIGHT
- 1—2'

FLOWERS
- a spike of dense, reddish purple flowers resembling elephant heads: the trunk is the upper petal, the "ears" are the lower lip petals

STEMS
- thick, erect, unbranched
- tinged with purple

LEAVES
- fern-like and pinnately divided
- sometimes tinged with purple

INDIAN USE
- carrot-like root was eaten raw or stewed

WILDLIFE USE
- grazing for elk

FELWORT - STAR SWERTIA

Swertia perennis
Gentian Family

HEIGHT
- ½—1½'

FLOWERS
- ¾'' wide, reddish purple, star-like flowers
- 5 petals, finely striped
- 2 hairy glands at the base of each petal

STEMS
- emerge from underground rhizomes

LEAVES
- mostly basal
- lanceolate and tapered
- pairs of leaves ascending the stem are smaller and clasping

FOUND
- moist meadows

BLOOMS
- July—September

SUGAR BOWL - VASE FLOWER
Clematis hirsutissima
Buttercup Family

FOUND
- moist soil of wooded areas and valleys

BLOOMS
- May—July

HEIGHT
- 1—2'

FLOWERS
- dark purple and nodding downwards
- no petals, but sepals are shaped like a sugar bowl
- sepals are covered with fine hairs, and tips curl backwards
- many stamens and pistils

STEMS
- hairy, and tend to be purplish near the bending top

LEAVES
- opposite, pinnately dissected, with very narrow and deeply cleft segments

INDIAN USE
- for medicinal purposes and, dried, as tinder to start fires

INTERESTING FACTS
- showy, feathery styles used in dried arrangements
- seeds very similar to those of "Prairie Smoke"

MONKSHOOD

Aconitum columbianum
Buttercup Family

HEIGHT
- 2—4'

FLOWERS
- blue-lavender and on a raceme
- 5 sepals resembling petals
- the upper sepal resembles the hood that gave the plant its name
- 2 side sepals are oval and broad, 2 lower sepals are narrow
- 2 petals are hidden under the "hood"

STEMS
- erect and sturdy

LEAVES
- 3—5, palmately lobed and deeply toothed

FOUND
- wet areas, streambanks
- usually in large patches

BLOOMS
- June—August

INTERESTING FACTS
- high alkaloid content
- **ENTIRE PLANT IS VERY POISONOUS!**

MERTENSIA - MOUNTAIN BLUEBELL
Mertensia ciliata
Borage Family

HEIGHT
• 1—4'

FLOWERS
• tubular, blue to lavender in color, in clusters, on stems that grow from upper axils
• 5 petals, 5 stamens, and 5 sepals, which together form a bell-shaped flower that droops

STEMS
• grow in clumps

LEAVES
• long, smooth, and lanceolate
• lower ones are are petioled

FOUND
• wet places, beside streams, and in meadows
• grows in clumps

BLOOMS
• June—August

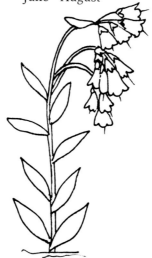

WILDLIFE USE
• elk seek bedding and birthing places where this plant grows
• deer, elk, bear, and domestic sheep feed on this plant
• pikas, animals that hide among the rocks and are known for their peeping sounds, harvest, dry, and store this plant for winter

ALPINE SPEEDWELL

Veronica wormskjoldii
Figwort Family

HEIGHT
- 3—6''

FLOWERS
- tiny and bluish lavender, growing together on a short raceme
- 4 unevenly shaped petals
- 2 stamens

STEMS
- very hairy and sticky

LEAVES
- lanceolate and opposite, clasping the stem

FOUND
- boggy meadows at high altitudes

BLOOMS
- June—August

INTERESTING FACT
- these tiny, blue flowers can almost always be found on trails leading to high mountain lakes

LUPINE

Lupinus sp.
Pea Family

INTERESTING FACTS
- hybridizes easily, therefore difficult to distinguish between species
- over 600 species have been identified
- "Blue Bonnet" (one of the blue species) is the state flower of Texas
- follows sun's path, closes at night

FOUND
- moist soils on hillsides and meadows
- some species found in dry, sandy soil

BLOOMS
- June—August

HEIGHT
- 1—2'

FLOWERS
- predominately blue in color, but also found in pink, yellow, or white
- 5 petals: 1 large broad upper petal, 2 side petals, and 2 lower petals that resemble a boat's keel
- grow in racemes
- similar to all flowers in the Pea Family
- seeds encased in a long, pod-like capsule

STEMS
- erect and sometimes branching

LEAVES
- alternate and mostly basal
- palmately compound, with 5 or more segments
- grey-green, smooth on top, and downy underneath

ROOTS
- deep taproot

Lupinus arbustus

PENSTEMON

Penstemon sp.
Figwort Family

HEIGHT
- ½—2′

FLOWERS
- many flowers growing on spikes or racemes
- tube-shaped corolla has 5 joined petals
- 2 upper lobes bend upwards, 3 lower lobes curve downwards
- 5 stamens, 1 with a tuft of hairs or "beard"

STEMS
- most species have several coarse stems that grow from a taproot

LEAVES
- paired, clasping, and in a variety of shapes
- basal leaves are larger than stem leaves
- sometimes lightly toothed

ROOTS
- taproot

FOUND
- high, moist mountain and sandy desert area
- some species grow in great profusion in mountain meadows

BLOOMS
- May—August

WILDLIFE USE
- some species eaten by sheep and other large animals

INTERESTING FACT
- over 200 species, mos found in the West
- also known as "Bearc tongues"
- found in a wide range of colors, mostly blue and white in the Rocky Mountains

HOT ROCK PENSTEMON—*Penstemon deustus*
Semi-shrub with whitish flowers, grows in dry soil, and has toothed leaves.

SHOWY PENSTEMON—*Penstemon speciosus*
One of the taller penstemons, it grows in moist, sandy soil,
and has a profusion of brilliant blue flowers up to 2″ long.

BUSH PENSTEMON—*Penstemon fruticosus*
This low-growing shrub is found in dry, rocky places.
Bright lavender flowers grow on one side of the stem; leaves are lanceolate.

BLUE CAMAS
Camassia quamash
Lily Family

INDIAN USE
- bulb was an important food source
- eaten raw, boiled, or roasted
- potato-like flavor
- ground into flour for bread
- this nutritious bulb was the cause of many Indian wars in areas where harvesting rights were strongly defended

WILDLIFE USE
- deer and elk graze on this plant in early spring

INTERESTING FACT
- many places are named after this important food source

HEIGHT
- 1—2'

FLOWERS
- bright blue flowers on a spike
- 3 sepals and 3 petals (appear to be 6 petals)
- 6 bright yellow stamens

STEMS
- unbranched

LEAVES
- basal and grass-like

BULB
- oval-shaped, about 1'' wide

FOUND
- in boggy meadows

BLOOMS
- April—June

LARKSPUR

Delphinium nelsonii
Buttercup Family

HEIGHT
- ½—2'

FLOWERS
- deep purple, and growing in a loose formation on a single raceme
- 4 petals, 5 sepals (all the same color)
- upper sepal is spurred

STEMS
- unbranched

LEAVES
- mostly basal and palmately lobed

ROOT
- tuber

FOUND
- widely distributed
- dry mountain valleys and ridges to sagebrush country

BLOOMS
- May—July

INTERESTING FACTS
- high alkaloid content
- toxicity decreases as plant matures
- **VERY POISONOUS TO GRAZING ANIMALS (EXCEPT DOMESTIC SHEEP)**

MOUNTAIN GENTIAN
Gentiana calycosa
Gentian Family

FOUND
- high altitudes
- boggy meadows
- grows in clumps

BLOOMS
- July—August

INTERESTING FACTS
- "Fringed Gentian" is the official flower of Yellowstone National Park
- because of its reputed medicinal value, it has been used as a tonic from ancient times

HEIGHT
- 3—15''

FLOWERS
- brilliant blue petals
- mostly single, but occasionally 3 to a stem
- upward facing, bell shaped
- 5 pointed petals, each connected by a pleated membrane
- stamens are shorter than the petals

STEMS
- branched near the ground
- each stem holds a single flower

LEAVES
- opposite, ovate, and shiny
- 3 prominent veins
- get larger as they grow up the stem

STICKSEED - FALSE FORGET-ME-NOT

Hackelia patens
Borage Family

HEIGHT
- 2—4′

FLOWERS
- tubular corolla spreads into 5 blue-lavender petals
- a white ring surrounds the tube opening
- the yellow center contains 5 stamens

STEMS
- small clusters of flowers are on curving stalks
- hairy

LEAVES
- lanceolate and narrow
- mostly basal leaves, growing smaller as they near the top

FOUND
- moist to medium-dry soils
- aspen groves

BLOOMS
- June—July

INTERESTING FACT
- flower seeds ripen into four nutlets, each with many barbs that cling to humans and animals for dispersal

SHRUBS WITH BERRIES

OREGON GRAPE
Mahonia repens
Barberry Family

LEAVES
- are compound, evergreen and leatherly
- holly-like with spiney toothed edges
- some turn red in the fall

STEMS
- underground runners produce offshoots

INDIAN USE
- roots and stems used as a bitter tonic
- yellow dye made from the stems of this plant
- was used for clothing and baskets

FOUND
- in dry soil of hills and woods

BLOOMS
- April—July

HEIGHT
- approximately 1′

FLOWERS
- small yellow clusters
- has 6 petals and 6 sepals

WILDLIFE USE
- black bears forage on this berry

INTERESTING FACTS
- at least 6 species of this plant in the Rocky Mountains
- also known as "Holly Grape" or "Mountain Holly"
- used to make jelly

ELDERBERRY
Sambucus coerulea
Honeysuckle Family

FOUND
- moist, wet soil
- open valleys up to 9,000'

HEIGHT
- 3—10'

BLOOMS
- June and July

FLOWERS
- numerous small, white flowers growing in a cluster of cymes

BERRIES
- abundant clusters of blue-black berries
- ripen in late August—October

STEMS
- reddish-brown in color
- filled with a spongelike substance
- snap easily

LEAVES
- opposite, pinnately divided and lanceolate
- edges are finely toothed

INDIAN USE
- bark and leaves used as a diuretic

WILDLIFE USE
- elk, deer and sheep forage on tender shoots
- berries attract birds

INTERESTING FACTS
- berries highly nutritious
- used for making wine and jelly

CHOKECHERRY
Prunus melanocarpa
Rose Family

FOUND
- along streams and in moist areas

HEIGHT
- can be a small shrub or a tree up to 20'

FLOWERS
- white or sometimes pinkish
- found on lateral branches
- grow in racemes
- have 5 petals
- prominent stamen

BLOOMS
- May—early July

BERRIES
- dark red and cherry-shaped
- have a hard center stone
- bitter taste
- ripen in the fall

STEMS
- young shoots growing from older branches

LEAVES
- alternate, elongated and ovate in shape
- finely toothed edges

INDIAN USE
- used fresh or dried in pemican

WILDLIFE USE
- sheep and mountain goats eat the stems and leaves
- birds feast on the berries

INTERESTING FACTS
- fruit is used for making syrup and jellies

WILD STRAWBERRY
Fragaria virginiana
Rose Family

HEIGHT
- 2—7"

FLOWERS
- 5 white petals, 5 green sepals, about 20 yellow stamens, and many yellow pistils
- prominent seeds are sunken into the fleshy fruit

STEMS
- short and spreading

LEAVES
- basal and with 3 segments
- outer parts of leaves are wider and toothed to about midpoint

FOUND
- moist soils, meadows, streams, and woods

BLOOMS
- May—August

ROOTS
- runners are generally above ground and produce new plants

INDIAN USE
- as well as eating the fruit, Indians brewed a tea from the leaves

WILDLIFE USE
- berries eaten by birds, rodents, and bears

INTERESTING FACTS
- rich in Vitamin C
- berries occur more often in the lower altitudes, where it is warmer and the growing season is longer

BLACK TWINBERRY
Lonicera involucrata
Honeysuckle Family

FOUND
- in moist places along streams and in woods

HEIGHT
- 3—6′

FLOWERS
- trumpet-shaped and grow at the ends of the branches
- pale yellow
- prominent stamen

BLOOMS
- end of May—June

BERRIES
- found usually in August and September
- black-colored berries surrounded by dark red bracts

STEMS
- brownish-grey branches turning light green where the flowers grow

LEAVES
- long and opposite
- ovate to lanceolate in shape

WILDLIFE USE
- bears, grouse and sheep forage on these berries

INTERESTING FACTS
- 5 species found in the Rocky Mountains
- not recommended for eating

SNOWBERRY
Symphoricarpos occidentalis
Honeysuckle Family

FOUND
- in mountain thickets and high desert prairies

HEIGHT
- 3—6′

FLOWERS
- white or pink
- grow in terminal spikes
- petals in a bell-shaped corolla
- 4—5 lobed bracts

BLOOMS
- June and July

BERRIES
- white and globular with two seeds
- harvested in late August and September

STEMS
- brown, bushy, branched and smooth

LEAVES
- deciduous and oval-shaped

WILDLIFE USE
- many animals graze on the young branches

INTERESTING FACTS
- a closely related and domesticated species is the *racemosus sp.*, also known as the "Snowball Tree"

RASPBERRY
Rubus idaeus
Rose Family

FOUND
- along streams and disturbed areas

HEIGHT
- 2—5'

FLOWERS
- white with 5 petals, numerous stamen and 5 sepals
- grow on lateral branches

BLOOMS
- late May, June and July

BERRIES
- red and thimble-shaped
- fall off coned-shaped receptacle when ripe
- harvested in late August and September

LEAVES
- 3 lobed and alternate
- deeply veined
- serrated edges
- lighter green underneath and hairy

STEMS
- long, arching and prickly canes

INDIAN USE
- an important part of their diet

WILDLIFE USE
- deer and bears forage on these berries

INTERESTING FACTS
- approximately 15 species in the Rocky Mountains
- one variety *(R. spectabilis)* has pink to lavender flowers with yellowish to light red berries

GOLDEN CURRANT

Ribes aureum
Gooseberry Family

FOUND
- near streams and hillsides

HEIGHT
- 3—10'

FLOWERS
- grow in racemes
- 5 bright yellow petals
- tubular with a spicy fragrance

BLOOMS
- late April to June

BERRIES
- are yellow-orange, reddish or occasionally black
- harvested in August and September

STEMS
- smooth

LEAVES
- alternate, lobed and palmate in shape
- smooth

INDIAN USE
- used for making pemican

WILDLIFE USE
- bear, deer, rodents and elk all forage on these berries

INTERESTING FACTS
- over 25 varieties in the Rocky Mountains
- "Sticky Currant" *(R. viscosissimum)* is sticky to the touch
- "Squaw Currant" *(R. cereum) has* waxy, insipid, orange berries
- many varieties make wonderful jelly

SERVICEBERRY
Amalanchier alnifolia
Rose Family

FOUND
- along streams and hillsides

HEIGHT
- 3—15' or more

FLOWERS
- white with 5 twisted and narrow petals

BLOOMS
- May—June

BERRIES
- dark bluish-purple
- almost 1/2" in diameter
- edible and sweet
- contain a few small soft seeds
- ripen the end of August to the middle of October

STEMS
- thornless

LEAVES
- oval and 1—2" long
- slightly toothed near the tip

WILDLIFE USE
- all parts of the plants eaten by many animals

INTERESTING FACTS
- delicious when made into a pie, jelly or wine

HUCKLEBERRY—GROUSEBERRY
Vaccinium scoparium
Heath Family

FOUND
- in moist areas under conifers (mostly lodgepole pines)

HEIGHT
- 6 1/2''—1 1/2'

FLOWERS
- vary from white to pink
- narrow and urn-shaped

BLOOM
- end of May—June

BERRIES
- small red berries ripening in July and August
- not too abundant
- a single berry grows from a leaf axis

STEMS
- branched and bushy

LEAVES
- small and oval in shape
- light green

THIMBLEBERRY
Rubus parviflorus
Rose Family

FOUND
- moist places

HEIGHT
- 2—6'

BLOOMS
- May—July

FLOWERS
- white with 7 to 10 petals up to 1 1/2'' across

BERRIES
- red and similar in looks to a raspberry
- not very flavorful
- harvested in August and September

STEMS
- lack prickles
- brownish
- shred as they mature

LEAVES
- 3—5 lobed and large (up to 8'' wide)
- almost round and palmate
- lighter green underneath

NAMING OF PLANTS

A taxonomist names plants following rules provided by the International Code of Botanical Nomenclature. To avoid confusion throughout the world, there is only one botanical name for each plant. A binomial system of two names (the genus and species) is used. These names are usually Latin, since that was the language of the educated class when botany was first becoming a formal science. The genus part of the name is always capitalized, with the species written in lower case, and both are either italicized or underlined.

Plants are named by the family, genus, species, and variety to which they relate. Every species belongs to a genus, and every genus belongs to a family. Plants within each separate category share similar characteristics that other plants do not have. Refer to the page on Flower Families in this book for examples. The Rose Family includes the genera rose, but also chokecherry, cinquefoil, and current. Each genus has similar characteristics that others do not have and is grouped together separately within the family.

The problem with using common names for plants is that the same plant may have many different names, or the same common name may apply to two different plants. "Bluebells" in Idaho refers to *Mertensia* plants, and, in Wyoming, to *Campanula,* for example.

Genus and species names are based on:

1. discoverers	5. mythology
2. description	6. medicinal properties
3. honorary merit	7. other reasons
4. geographic location	

For example, *Fragaria idahoensis* tells us that the plant comes from Idaho and is fragrant. *Pinus edulis* means edible in reference to the pinenuts from this pine tree.

CHARACTERISTICS OF FLOWER FAMILIES
MENTIONED IN THIS BOOK

BORAGE: Flowers are symmetrical; 5 petals, 5 sepals, and 5 stamens united at the base into a narrow tube that flares at the top. Plants are generally covered with hairs, and flowers often grow on one side of the stem. Leaves are simple (not compound). Four seed-like nutlets.

BUCKWHEAT: Many small flowers in involucre clusters. No true petals. 4—6 sepals, 6—9 stamens. Leaves are basal, and surround swollen nodes. Superior ovary with a 2- or 3-parted style.

BUTTERCUP: Usually 5 petals and 5 sepals. Numerous stamens. Leaves generally alternate, and are usually palmately divided.

COMPOSITE: Flower heads usually consist of outer ray flowers and center disk flowers, are radically symmetrical, and are surrounded by a ring of green bracts. Fine hairs (pappus) grow between the bracts and the petals. Inferior ovary. Leaves are simple or compound, alternate or opposite.

EVENING PRIMROSE FAMILY: Flowers are clustered on racemes or spikes, with 4 petals, 4 sepals, and 4—8 stamens. Inferior ovary. Leaves can be alternate or opposite.

FIGWORT: Flowers are bilaterally symmetrical. 4—5 petals are united, and 4—5 sepals are united to form a corolla. 4—5 stamens. Corolla has upper and lower lips (like a snapdragon). Leaves alternate, opposite, whorled and/or pinnately divided.

FLAX: Slender-stemmed plants. 5 petals, 5 sepals, 10 stamens. Leaves are alternate or opposite and thread-like.

GENTIAN: 4—5 petals and 4—5 sepals are all fused at the base, forming a tube-shaped corolla. 4—5 stamens are also fused to the corolla. Ovary superior. 1 style. Leaves are opposite.

GERANIUM: 5 petals, 5 sepals, 5—15 stamens. Ovary superior. Fruit develops from a long beak-like pistil. Leaves are mainly palmately lobed and deeply cleft.

HEATH: 4—5 petals and 4—5 sepals, both united. Twice as many sepals. Flowers are globe-shaped. Leaves are alternate, leathery, and evergreen. A shrub.

HONEYSUCKLE: Many branched shrub with white to pinkish flowers and white, waxy berries. Generally 5 petals in a bell-shaped corolla.

HYDRANGEA: Deciduous shrub with 4—10 petals, 4—10 sepals, and many stamens. Flowers are radially symmetrical. Leaves are ovate and opposite.

LILY: Sepals and petals in 3's and the same color. Mostly 6 stamens. All parts are attached to the base of a superior ovary. Leaves are basal, alternate, and linear. Flowers grow in racemes or spikes.

LOASACEAE: Shrub with bristly hairs on leaves. Flowers grow either singly or on a cyme and are yellow to orange in color. 4—5 petals with many stamen.

MALLOW: 5 petals, 3—5 sepals, numerous stamens. All parts are attached to the base of superior ovary. Leaves are alternately and palmately lobed. Hairy stem.

MINT: Flowers are bilaterally symmetrical. 5 petals and 5 sepals (all united), 2—4 stamens. Stems are square, leaves opposite or whorled. Ovary of 4 nutlets. Mint aroma.

ORCHID: Showy flowers, bilaterally symmetrical. 3 petals (2 side and 1 prominent lip), 3 sepals, 1—2 stamens joined together with the pistil into a column. Inferior ovary. Leaves alternate.

PARSLEY: Aromatic plant. 5 petals, 5 sepals, 5 stamens. Flowers are radially symmetrical umbels. Carrot-like leaves alternate, pinnately compound.

PEA: Irregularly shaped flower with 5 petals (1 large upper petal, 2 side wing petals and 2 lower ones joined to resemble a boat's keel), 5 sepals, 10 stamens. Ovary superior. Seeds contained in a long pod. Tendrils. Leaves pinnately or palmately divided and sometimes simple.

PEONY: Shrub with large showy flowers. 5—10 petals, 5 sepals, many stamens, 2—5 separate pistils. Leaves are alternate and divided.

PHLOX: 5 petals, 5 sepals, 5 stamens (all parts connected to the base of the ovary). Trumpet-shaped corolla branches into 5 lobes. Flowers grow singly or in a cyme. Leaves are alternate or opposite, simple or compound. Can be prickly.

PINK: 5 petals, 5 sepals, 5—10 stamens. Grow singly or in a cluster. Leaves are simple and opposite. Stems can have swollen nodes.

PURSLANE: Radially symmetrical. 4 or more petals, 2 or more sepals, many stamens. Ovary mostly superior. Leaves are simple and alternate or opposite in a basal rosette, somewhat succulent.

ROSE: Flowers are radially symmetrical. 5 petals, 5 sepals, numerous stamens. Ovary is partially inferior. Thorny stem. Leaves are simple, alternate and compound. A pair of prominent stipules is usually present at the base of leaf petiole.

SAXIFRAGE: Flowers are regular and very delicate. 5 petals, 5 sepals, 5—10 stamens growing in a raceme. Superior to semi-inferior ovary. Leaves are mostly basal and alternate.

STONECROP: Succulent. Flowers grow in cymes. 4—5 petals, 4—5 sepals, 4—5 pistils, twice as many stamens. Compact, whorled leaves.

VALERIAN: Bilaterally symmetrical. 5 petals (sometimes have a prominent spur), sepals obscure, 1—4 stamens. Ovary is inferior. Leaves are basal and opposite, mostly pinnately divided.

VIOLET: Irregularly shaped. 5 petals (2 upper petals, 2 side petals, and a lower spurred petal), 5 sepals, 5 stamens. Ovary is superior. Leaves are basal, alternate, slightly toothed and mostly on stems.

WINTERGREEN: Radially symmetrical. Low, evergreen plant. 4—5 united petals, 4—5 sepals, 10 stamens are all attached to a superior ovary and growing in branched clusters. Leaves are alternate and somewhat whorled.

COMMON NAMES INDEX

BOTANICAL NAMES INDEX

BIBLIOGRAPHY

Craighead, John J.; Craighead, Frank C.; Davis, Ray J. *A Field Guide to Rocky Mountain Wild Flowers*. Houghton-Mifflin Co. Boston, MA. 1963.

Cronquist, Arthur. *Intermountain Flora, Vol. 5*. New York Botanical Gardens. Bronx, New York. June 30, 1994.

Hitchcock, C. Leo; Cronquist, Arthur. *Flora of the Pacific Northwest*. University of Washington Press. Seattle and London. 1973.

McDorman, Bill. *High Altitude Gardens Catalog*. Ketchum, ID. 1998.

Niehaus, Theodore F. and Ripper, Charles L. *Pacific States Wildflowers*. Houghton Mifflin Company. Boston, MA. 1976.

Ornduff, Robert. *Introduction to California Plant Life*. University of California Press. Berkeley, CA. 1974.

Peterson, Lee Allen. *Edible Wild Plants*. Houghton Mifflin Company. Boston, MA. 1977.

Rickett, Harold William. *Wild Flowers of the United States, Vol. 6, The Central Mountains and Plains*. McGraw-Hill Book Co. New York, NY. 1973.

St. John, Harold. *Flora of Southeastern Washington and Adjacent Idaho*. Lancaster Press, Inc. Lancaster, PA. 1939.

Scotter, George W. and Flygare, Haille. *Wildflowers of the Canadian Rockies*. Hurtig Publishers Ltd. Edmonton, Alberta, Canada. 1986.

Shaw, Richard J. *Plants of Yellowstone and Grand Teton National Parks*. Wheelwright Press, Ltd. Salt Lake City, UT. 1981.

Shaw, Richard J. and On, Danny. *Plants of Waterton-Glacier National Parks*. Mountain Press Publishing Company. Missoula, MT. 1979.

Spellenberg, Richard. *The Audubon Society Field Guide to North American Wildflowers, Western Region*. Alfred A. Knopf, Inc. New York, NY. 1979.

Strickler, Dr. Dee. *Alpine Wildflowers*. The Flower Press. Columbia Falls, MT. 1990.